SING SOLO BARITONE

—Edited by John Carol Case—

First published by Oxford University Press 1985
Revised edition published 1986

1. THE SONG OF MOMUS TO MARS

from 'A Secular Masque' (1750)

John Dryden
(1631–1700)

WILLIAM BOYCE
(1711–79)

Piano accompaniment by G.E.P. Arkwright

Piano accompaniment © Oxford University Press 1927. Renewed in U.S.A. 1955

This edition © Oxford University Press 1985

Printed in Great Britain

OXFORD UNIVERSITY PRESS, MUSIC DEPARTMENT, WALTON STREET, OXFORD OX2 6DP

4

Fools are on-ly thin-ner, With all our Cost and Care; But nei — ther Side a _ Win-ner, For Things are as they_ were,

[echo _ _ _ _ _ _ _ _ _]

Things are as they_ were, Things are _ as they were; The

Fools are _ on-ly _ thin-ner, With all our_ Cost and_ Care;_ But

Sing Solo (Baritone)

2. CORPUS CHRISTI CAROL

(1961)

arranged by the composer from 'A Boy was Born'

Anon
(15th cent.)

BENJAMIN BRITTEN
(1913–76)

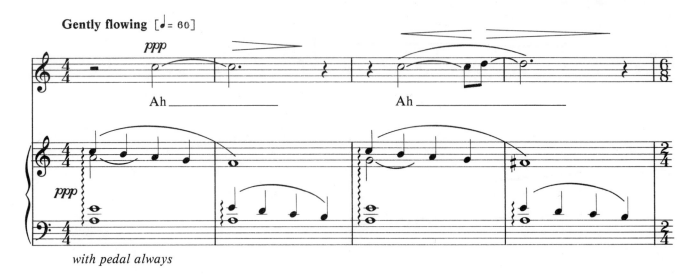

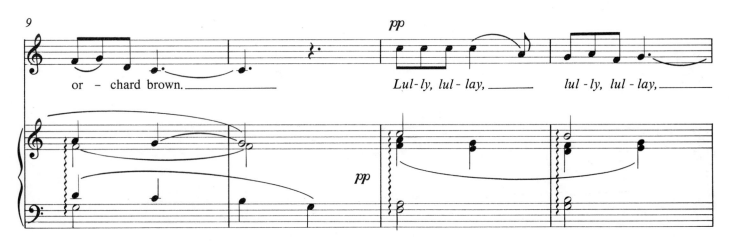

¹mate

The fal-con hath borne __ my make __ a - way.

And by that bed -- side there stand-eth a stone, __

Cor - pus Chris-ti writ-ten there-on. __ Ah __

Ah __

3. FELDEINSAMKEIT

Op.86 No.2

Hermann Allmers
(1821–1902)
Translation by John Carol Case

JOHANNES BRAHMS
(1833–97)

12

4. AN EPITAPH

Walter de la Mare*
(1873–1956)

IVOR GURNEY
(1890–1937)

*Marion M. Scott writes in the Preface to the complete volume:
"When setting . . . . he [Gurney] depended almost entirely on memory. As a
result he did not always reproduce each word with literal exactness.
. . . . wherever Gurney's differed from the poets' own versions the latter have
been added in small type below."
J.C.C. adds: In performance, I always sang the small type.

Original key: D major

– er was _____ in _ the West Coun-try. _____

But beau – ty pass – es; beau – ty van-ish-es;

van – ish-es; pass – es;

How - ev - er rare, ____ rare ____ it be; ____

5. WANDERERS NACHTLIED

Johann Wolfgang von Goethe
(1749–1832)

D.768 (1823)

FRANZ SCHUBERT
(1797–1828)

Translation by A. H. Fox Strangways and Steuart Wilson

schwei-gen im__ Wal — de. War — te nur, war — te nur,
end - ed their__ mel - o - dy. Wait a while, wait a while,

cresc.

bal — de ru – hest du auch. War — te nur,
one ____ day You too shall sleep. Wait a while,

pp

war – te nur, bal – de ru – hest du auch.
wait a while, one__ day You too shall sleep.

cresc. *p* *pp*

6. THE LARK IN THE CLEAR AIR

Irish Air
Arr. PHYLLIS TATE
(b.1911)

Sir Samuel Ferguson
(1810–86)

Dear thoughts are in my mind, and my soul soars enchanted As I hear the sweet lark sing in the clear air of the

day. For a ten - der beam-ing smile to my

hope has been grant - ed, And to - mor - row she shall

hear all my fond heart would say.

[poco piu mosso]

I shall tell her all my

Sing Solo (Baritone)

7. SLEEP

John Fletcher
(1579–1625)

PETER WARLOCK
(1894–1936)

To be sung as though unbarred, *i.e.* phrased according to the natural
accentuation of the words, especially avoiding an accent on the first beat of
the bar when no accent is demanded by the sense.

long an-noy, Are con — tent — ed with a thought Thro' an i – dle fan – cy wrought:

O _____ let my joys have some a – bi – ding.

8. VOUCHSAFE, O LORD

from 'Dettingen Te Deum' (1743)

G. F. HANDEL
(1685–1759)

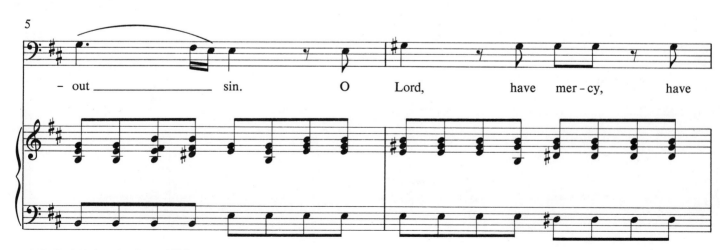

9. SCHON EILET FROH DER AKKERSMANN

WITH JOY THE IMPATIENT HUSBANDMAN

Gottfried van Swieten
(1734–1803)

from 'Die Jahreszeiten' (1800)

The Seasons

F. J. HAYDN
(1732–1809)

Translation based on James Thomson's poem

Simon

Schon ei - let froh der
With joy th'im - pa - tient

Ak - kersmann zur__ Ar - beit auf das Feld, in lan - gen Fur - chen schrei - tet er dem
hus-band-man Drives forth his lus-ty team To where the well-us'd plough re-mains, Now

Haydn indicated phrasing and dynamics in the instrumental parts only, but
these should also be followed by the singer.

Original key: C major

53
ab - ge - mess-nem Gan - ge dann, in ab - ge - mess-nem Gan - ge dann wirft
mea-sur'd step he throws the grain, With mea-sur'd step he throws the grain with -

57
er den Sa - men aus, den_
- in the bounteous earth. O_

61
birgt der_ Ak - ker treu, den birgt der_ Ak - ker treu und reift ihn
sun, soft show'rs and dews! O_ sun, soft show'rs and dews! The gold - en

ten.

66
bald zur gold - nen Frucht, und reift
ears in plen - ty bring, The gold -

sempre p

Sing Solo (Baritone)

Sing Solo (Baritone)

10. PAPAGENO'S ARIA

from 'Die Zauberflöte' (1791)

The Magic Flute

Emanuel Schikaneder
(1751–1812)

Translation by E. J. Dent

W. A. MOZART
(1756–91)

English translation © Oxford University Press 1937

This edition © Oxford University Press 1985

Mozart gives no indication of phrasing or dynamics in the vocal-line: try to
follow the directions in the accompaniment.

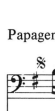

Papageno

1. Der Vo-gel - fän - ger bin ich ja, stets lu - stig, hei - sa! hop-sa-sa! ich
2. Der Vo-gel - fän - ger bin ich ja, stets hur - tig, hei - sa! hop-sa-sa! ich
1. *Now tell me, did you ev-er see So* *strange a kind of man as me? Yet*
2. *But there's a sport that's fi-ner yet Than traps for sil-ly birds to set; Yes,*

Vo - gel - fän - ger bin be - kannt bei alt und jung im gan - zen Land.
Vo - gel - fän - ger bin be - kannt bei alt und jung im gan - zen Land.
young and old__ in__ ev' - ry place Are al - ways glad to see my face.
bra - ver__ game there is, I know, And af - ter it I mean to go.

Weiss mit dem Lo - cken um - zu - geh'n, und
Ein__ Netz für Mäd - chen möch-te ich, ich
I __ spread my nets__ and__ whis - tle clear To
I'd __ glad - ly ply __ the __ fowl - er's trade If

Sing Solo (Baritone)

mich auf's Pfei - fen zu ver - steh'n!
fing sei dut - zend - weis für mich!
catch the birds as — they come near,
I could catch a — pret - ty maid.

Drum
Dann
And —
Then —

kann ich froh und lu - stig sein, denn al — le Mäd - chen sind ja — mein.
sperr - te ich — sie bei mir ein, und al — le Mäd - chen wä - ren — mein.
from this cage they can - not stir, For I'm the jol - ly — bird - catch - er.
who would share the — cage with her? Why, sure, the jol - ly — bird - catch - er!

11. LUNGI DAL CARO BENE

Cavatina
introduced in the opera 'Giulio Sabino'

English paraphrase by John Carol Case

G. SARTI
(1729–1802)

Lun - gi_ dal ca - ro be - ne,
Far from my dear be - lov - ed,

Vi - ve - re non poss'
How can_ I live with -

* ♩. ♪♬ may be performed ♩ ♪♩♩ , and similar adaptations made where appropriate.

Sing Solo (Baritone)

Reproduced and printed by
Halstan & Co. Ltd., Amersham, Bucks., England